The Wellsprings

25263

We all remember
Lengthened days
Brighter sky
Change of air
The certainly arriving Spring.
—Bertolt Brecht

Perhaps followers always sleep.
—Sherwood Anderson

Harry Lewis

The Wellsprings

Momo's Press   1981   San Francisco

Copyright © 1982 by Harry Lewis. All rights reserved.

This book was partially funded by grants from the California Arts Council, and the National Endowment for the Arts, a Federal Agency.

Some of these poems have appeared in # *and* Handbook *(magazines), and in* Babies, *a limited edition Little Rootie Tootie Book.*

All quotes from Wilhelm Reich in "The Wellsprings: A Suite For Wilhelm Reich and Thelonious Monk," are from The Function Of The Orgasm, *(New York, Pocket Books, 1975).*

Momo's Press
45 Sheridan Street
San Francisco,
CA 94103

Drawings and author photograph by Basil King.
Book design by Jon Goodchild.

First printing

Printed in the United States of America

Library of Congress Cataloging in Publication Data

Lewis, Harry, 1942-
The wellsprings.

I. Title.
PS3562. E945W4   811'.54   81-16762
ISBN 0-917672-18-6   AACR2
ISBN 0-917672-17-8 (pbk.)

for my mother: Sylvia Lewis

Contents

Love Poems and Situations
    The Roots of the Devil
    The Feeding
    Night
    If We Set Mothers Free To Set Us Free
    The New World
    Situations / 45
    Situations / 44
    Situations / 12
    Love Poem
    A Map of the Floor of the Oceans
    The New World
    The Map Made Clear . . .
    Another View of the Body
    Interpersonal Notes
    Situations / 2
    Situations / 10

***The Wellsprings:* A Suite for Thelonious Monk and Wilhelm Reich**
    1) *the long day*
    2) *on the creative*
    3) *the line*
    4) *conscious action is*
    5) *the function of the blues*
    6) *the archaeology of us*

A Portrait of Wilhelm Reich
    The Rich Soil / The Question / The Point
A Portrait of Thelonious Monk
    first solo
    second solo
    third solo

    7) *finale*

    Coda

Love Poems and Situations

The Roots
of the Devil

what?
the devil?
do I mean?
I mean
love
is
a long long
time a plant
growing sweet
around itself
can tangle its life
like
a root, I whisper
to my devil.
he whispers back
love is a dead plant. my devil
curls around that stem
                                his tail
in my heart to
                the very
                          root.
              it is
a knot
he insists
I will not cut. oh . . .
cut that knot
cut it:
      grow / grow
rootless in
the ether of angels.

The Feeding

the tenderness hurts—roots
oh
    rooted around
the stem
        out of doors
a constant hum
            against it
comes longing
          nibbling—*oh
do not touch no*
        tender—NO

            STOP
sweet—sometimes—so fine
I can almost taste—ah
there's
    the rub against it
until the lips crack with feeding
until that is
        tears—the eyes
rubbed red
      —it is a wonder
I wonder how
it still surfaces in me
—my mouth still ready
to suck as much as
I can get. —my eyes
wander at times wide
awake in the baby
pulling in
anything
I
can get.

Night

for William Carlos Williams and Victor Sobey (the good doctors)

1)

the child lays in the closed room does not go to sleep
lays in the dark
                —expectantly
off base
not knowing (what?)
                        was going to
                                    happen (?)
I must have wanted to cry
only
it wouldn't come. I must have remembered
a time when
            I cried.
            I must have felt it
all over me
driving me
to greater furies
until I sweated / fought
to surround myself with
its deafening
protection. I must have
heard myself
with astonishment
and satisfaction. I must have
bent
      back on
            my head
            and heels
                    yelling.
I know my mother was frightened
but could not touch me even when
she picked me up
waiting
        I must have wanted
that warmth. I must have been
surprised
            terrified in her cold arms.
when she put me down
I must have started

                        to yell
                        again
when she put me down.

2)

but
I want
to hear
myself
again.
I want to know
I am here. it is night
with its angry face
its loneliness that is
terrifying. my own voice
kills it / but
it comes again
if I stop. it is
less lonely
to yell. but
my voice seems
to have become part of
the dark. I want
to cry again
with my whole body.
I want my voice
to join my body.
I want an answer to
the cry. I want
that pleasure.

3.

we approach the end
in darkness
            —the mother of sleep
the worst misfortune of all. we are
driven away
into a place we have never seen. the darkness
falls / we go up
rapidly
through it. we cry
we sob
        scream
in blank terror. why doesn't someone

come? we reach out
expecting to be taken
by someone who
can break that dark. the night
stands outside the window. this time
it doesn't come in—but
it smiles: "see you later.
don't forget me."

If We Set Mothers Free
To Set Us Free

*there are no mothers
in
a patriarchy*

warriors
know nothing
about
      nurturing . . .
                no damn brats
   no
tenderness
        no way
              to hold close
no flesh
     that is not
MEAT.

     well
we do
the best we can.
we are cast out
against ourselves: in
a patriarchy
         babies are meat
                    in mama's arms
      as papa's eyes bulge
hungry: *give me some MEAT*
              MAMA
and she gives papa
the child
     all sweet
all ready
     for the grinder
at which point
the wound is salted
         and packed. it will
  never heal.

The New World

for Basil King

the idea delivered whole
is an awesome thing
                          roots
into our lives
reveals
       the need
               delivered
it claws
       breaks
              through our heads
we are the device
              through our heads
an open heart
            a sky
slow accumulation of clouds

                           a fragmented life is
a life of ideas
            that never take shape: polite society
makes ikons of the fragments:
                        fixed
                        to hold
each piece
as pure.
the idea
       delivered whole
is element
        / the whole cloud
floats

almost everyone I have spoken to for the last few weeks
is waiting for spring. for the last three days I have
been in bed waiting but today I went out / visited a friend
in Brooklyn
in his studio
          I saw a painting
that gave me SPRING

                        full
                                    about to bud. later
we drank
            ate dinner
with his whole family. I could taste spring. it was
a main course.

the idea delivered whole
is power
we will see
            what we
                        can do
                                    with it.
it is much easier
                        to add new twists to old ideas.
to make something new
                        means
there is
no other way. once
it is made
            you can turn away but
there is no turning back:

can blow fresh music
never a horn again after
                        what Louis licked
out of the blue ore like an olive branch not
pieces but made SOUND—never
a horn like that never again like that they
all heard it a whole new way a list after that
of those who played it and those who learned those
who moved
on that
            never a simple blues
after Parker made his own mistakes
whole the whole music hooting through
blues into BOP bang Parker was always
hungry HOOTING the blues like
a sweet cabbage soup I eat to fill me with this
saw Cézanne
            saw where the inside
                                    and the outside
            touched
watched the whole thing particularly
there was nothing else to talk about there was
everything else to see those eyes Brueghel
to a poetry in the streets of America made whole

whole (the cook is a doctor of what we are hungry
for) whole
           whole again wherever it is opened wholly
amazed
        always
                after the fact (no mere sum of parts: the addition
is over. gone mad with counting. gone too sure with all
the parts.) afraid (as always)
                               that anyone might see clearly
the poor man or woman crazed with that clear vision needing
some touch tender into the wild confusion that seeing something
(anything) whole
                 makes us difficult / quiet simply the body
streams with such clarity . . . that pleasure is a beginning
it is as my friend the painter has shown me. it is
possible in Brooklyn. it is possible anyplace. it is
a well-made meal. the cabbage soup gets better the more
you add to it the cat goes wild with the spices . . . cooking
swings through us. take a deep smell. look at the food
that's been made. look and listen

BUT DON'T STOP.
                 a phrase can be light
                        can be
                              aroma
                              stock
                              beef
                              cabbage
                              spice
                              color
                              sound
through every scale (the weight is not obvious) add mixed greens.
a soup is filling. starts with a simple idea. I WANT
TO MAKE A SOUP. or BREAD (a staple) how often Brueghel painted
people eating (or being eaten)
                               Bosch also
to the simple stew

                    to eat means
to make a meal. a stew is always delivered whole. the mind is
the cook. who's in the kitchen listening
                                         watching? who's looked
into the dining room recently and counted the people who are
waiting to be fed?

there is a woman
I went with her
through every old idea of love
we tried everything
faced with the fact that
we were breaking up
she reached out
she said:
we don't know what love is.
we are afraid. we try to make our ideas of love
take shape
    have feeling. we are
numb.
when we found ourselves in bed
later that night
I asked her
    how we could even know how
to hold each other.
we understood
that we would have to learn.

in my friend's painting
      (the one that brought me spring)
there was a birth. it took him three years
to deliver it.
   until about two months ago
the painting was trying to move between
hell

  the lower half (organic
       lover
        half)
life
 into
   heaven

    the upper half.

when the painting worked
there was
   no heaven
      and
  no hell

but
the entire world
full of juice

       —it was SPRING.

Situations / 45

                          a couple of drunks on the IRT
a young Spanish kid stoned
an old man
          grayhaired
                    no clear age
both
     half asleep (blind
                 pissed) and
                          otherwise
out. they surface in fragments at
local stops. leave
              at 34th street
        Penn Station
sweet
the old man takes
the young man's hand
                  and leads him out.

Situations / 44

for C.

the joys of summer love
my lady grabbing me warm lush
rubbing my cock
               in the doorway
                         in
             the summer
I'll always love
             that light summer rain
searching for her ears
             the light tingle of
her musty taste—it is
DELIGHT . . .
             a pleasure
to give myself to her
in a dream
no future
             no place but
her body
             her hand on me in a doorway
my hard cock striking
                   lightning in my pants
all perfect
         right
             down to
the promise
             of an intimate dinner
come (and again)
Monday night—oh
             the charm of
such lust . . .

Situations / 12

a thin woman walks through the waiting room of the doctor's office
counting each step
                       as pain
hangs up
          her coat
                   comes back
                              sits down
                                     next to me
I am ready to scream
                   she hurts so much.

she takes out
              a small mirror
makes up her face for
the doctor
              her breathing
the whole room's
                   thick
everybody
              breathing.
this woman has no body
white skin
              pale red
                      through the surface
              she is almost
pure
surface
        lets out
              air. she is flat.
          her toes
move
her toes are alive
                   all her life in
those toes
          in
              her open shoes
wiggling
          for dear life. she coughs

    her body
            takes new
                      shape
            settles
back
      to long tight breath / she fixes
      her hair for
                the doctor
her toes
cough.

Love Poem

for Nana

moaning
and groaning
our nights
and our days
our couplings
particular
        practical
                joy: I think of you
        under me
or on top of me
a voice that fills us
making that point
            and we
                insist on it.
                I think of you
            with me
moaning
a pleasure
        we groan
the hold takes fast
into the shape we tangle in then
thinking
      of
         others: how
         they too
      must fill the air 'round
them
     those friends
              who love the sound
              and those
     who fear the sound keeping
as I have known
           and you have known
that silence
        that hand which pushes in
stops the breath dead
            in the body.
           —how

do they? how do we keep
pleasure full to our days
       hold off
the things our fears create
to stop the lush-life filling us? there are
        days
I wake up early in the morning
hear people scream into the streets
that they've
been tied up
    gagged
       and robbed (that moan
       is not
    what I want morning
to make) but
also mornings when
I have heard others wail exactly
their voices lovers into sunlight
at nights
in a moon moan of what dream holds them tight
friends (there are two I have in mind) have been
together now
      seventeen years
and still make
    that real sound
    their children
learn from them
     that joy. their bodies bud
     open
and answer
    says
that sound we make is right:
a family teaches the young
      pleasure
not the business of pleasure but
making a full deep sound in
       our bodies:
       it is there when
we come
  hold
    move each other: but
    how it stops
      in the dead air
      our world makes
     fear (how will we feed ourselves?
where are our clothes)—what revolution can
we hope for now
     that does not kill?

                              except as
                              we hold
                    moan
hold pleasure
                    —ask nothing
but to hold
             damn tight
                         ourselves fast
in each other: to build a nation on that
(for days now
I keep saying to myself YES
build a NATION on the soft tender groan
build a politics of that—an economics
of that low sweet moan
build a real nation between such bodies
such needs
            as hold us
                       together).
do not take this for a clever image or
a metaphor
            —but for
                     the flesh it is
a way to write history
and talk to each other. I am
no dreamer. I don't do well
with dreams—but want to take this
to the heart
insist
      that
           when I think of you
(or any woman
              or any man
              in that embrace)
it is
    a real world
    I see
and hear.

A Map of the Floor of the Oceans

for Charles Mingus — passing January 8, 1979

we all
      each of us
have always been
in love
      have always been
the oceans' floor
            backbone
fine
    fine music in a deep note
passing

      and who will say
the moves
         a man makes (among us)
are not passing fine
         while
             going through
I mean   Mingus'
        run — how many times
back
    in the curve of
        the piano
he demanded
      perfection
           in the fire of
                the time
          a terror
      a pure
hard
   joy

      and who will say
the changes a man calls
          are not his moods
many
     and gliding (rippling
            under oceans

making a floor as
            his ashes settle there)
there
where there are more
                many more
than three or four
incarnations of
a lovebird.

The New World

for George Grosz

not only pictures out by that gone world
not that gone this
man having made
second world war
come / over again
we start first a man
next to me by my bed
box head
        stub body
bites his cigar / black eyes
stench
        touches my tits
fingers my gentle soft sweet flesh sweet
girl body—DO NOT DEFILE ME
my pure charm gentle
innocence
        silk hair over my
slit. dirty man. DO NOT DARE
he puts on a new dress
        uniform
I have grown a small mustache
        below my nose
it wiggles it jiggles: the glorious state.
pure state. beautiful race
DO NOT DARE DEFILE. mommy

daddy
    come
        soothe me
caress in the backs of their minds
the years I was their second born
tranquil marriage in my
youth gentle artist
        love
do not
defile nothing but
it explodes. I sit up
cover my tits—no more milk for the children
the marriage is over / life
always at dawn / marriages
in doorways over bars. I am
the bartender

giving booze-milk into wee small
hours. my bra is transparent
my dress is the man
                      the armies
to protect by words
pure man—it's given to the hands
of the huge doorman
                      fezzed
bearded. does not die
unless he wants to / thousands of
knives guns emptied into him
he stands over the room / comes
at me strips me sticks
his fencepost into my wet
slash. DO NOT DEFILE ME. do not
dare. my heat sets fire to the world
oven of purity
blast furnace of hermaphrodite
booze: I bar
tender woman I
world bearer of men. I have given up
all for the good of Man. I am such
virile body such hard body. the delight
of all women. we come in. I serve us.
we take a table. I play
the juke
box
    bar
in full swing
           my hand touches
                          my tits
           across
from me
       my hand
             comes back
       from me
to caress my prick.
more drinks.
the world will not end.
I world
am beautiful this tender
man / woman the bar (when it is empty)
at morning there are
the leavings of last night's
sure thing
to be cleaned for the coming
night / the new world
again and
again.

The Map Made Clear When Suddenly Faced with Seeing An Old Lover and Feeling It Deeply One Night Before A Meeting / The Fear of That and the Need To Feel My Body Change As It Moves

1.

there's a cartography of . . .
of the body
a body of weight
                        leads to (all roads to)
the heart
       for
              that matter
I hardly remember my last lover
but suddenly my body tingles
with a lover I haven't seen in 8 years:
I began to cry tonight
                        remembering her
in my body
         (her mouth on me
to an orgasm that knocked me out)
in my stomach
                that fear that I could do nothing
remembering how coldly she cut me off
                                how perfect
that romance was

                8 years later crying because
I am meeting her for a drink tomorrow
afternoon. crying because
I am afraid / I remember that feeling as my stomach
tightens
            as my groin locks
as my throat catches
my bowels press out:
                        that map.

2.

every few months
I change my face:
recently
        I cut my beard (looked young again)
now
    my mustache is coming back (the hair on
my neck stands on end sometimes if I breathe
deeply . . .)
              it's getting clear
                        the best (maybe)
the only love poems
                are written when
you're in love (the love poem is a cartography of
bodies) the rest is
                sad stuff
                        we settle for
like broken hearts (a broken heart
            tears the map / all the poems
            all the tears
                    can't put it back
        together again)
sad stuff
        a lot of paste for broken-hearted
melodies (used to joke about it . . .
                            oh well
so it didn't work out
at least
        I got
            a few
                love poems out of it . . .)
no one laughs. who the hell was I kidding
so

I feel my body each day
change my face once-in-a-while (the long

```
        the short
                the fat
                        thin of it
                                hair of my chin
                        under my nose
down onto my back)
                        I feel my body each day
try a different look
                        consider new roads into
through
        to
from
my heart: that's
my science.
```

Another View of the Body

There is not much knowledge that leads to power, but plenty of knowledge to which only power can lead.
—Bertolt Brecht

1.

all my science
                all my body
still breaks—reaches
                          desperately for deep breath
or in that breath
                an easing into love / but then
just when
       I thought
                I was in control (such knowledge
such power)
        —my liver broke
devouring my energy
                    scaring me (my eyes
                    gone
yellow)
      a fever going up
                       down (I became
       my own thermometer)
seeing the picture on my walls breathing
I dreamt a science
              that would give
sure knowledge—I dreamt
I could read it in
          my liver—the liver
become iron—rusted
oh—what science
              will give love?

2.

each day
      I nurse my liver
                back to health.

every other day
            I go to the fancy little butcher:
he takes out a calf's liver
                    cuts slowly
                            silent
                        like butter. each day
I feed
        my liver
                liver.

3.

everything
        around me
is cut to order (in an age of
great discoveries and inventions
                            you
                                must have
                            an inclination
to penetrate
            things).

Interpersonal Notes

for Eleanor Burke Leacock

1.

the dehumanization
of conjugal relationships
men and women
              caught
                      as we are . . .
the network of fear
confusion. (the woman
I love and who
              loves me. she writes
a letter
      affirming
              from a distance
her love. she tells me how hard it is
to give that love when we are
together. it is also
easier for me to write letters
or poems to her
              using that romance
to keep us distant . . . there is so little / some fragments
of a holding when we are together) that romance:

the petty dominance of the man (I resist her will
or give in petulant) the anger and bitterness of
the woman (she finds it hard to be tender
even when she wants to give that gift . . .) all too often
a constant battle. all this is only too well
known.

2.

looking back can also be
a romance.
            it is the breakdown
            here. the failure

here
      in our daily lives
forces the longing (despite
the fact that preclass societies
have already been undercut by
European and American
colonization—colonized by
our fear
      confusion
            our bitterness
or need
colonized by our
longing—despite that fact
we find in what still remains
after we have broken their lives
a quality of
respectful ease—never absolute
or pure—but present
a warmth
an assurance in personal contact) it is
still there
like a ghost
persists as evidence
that the tensions in our lives
are not in the natures of
men and women.

Situations / 2

the day started with my friends
the ones who are a family
I woke with the voices of
the children: their mother
the two girls preparing for their day
the mother for her day—the
chatter / the quick outbreaks
angry looking for little things
to take to school or
the office—there's
a love
about the whole thing.
it is a morning. I listen
get up slowly
          get into my pants

go out to it. we eat
a light breakfast
talk. it is as if I was
the father. even when
my friend
the father comes down it does not
change. it is the family
opens
     a lesson
          —how days start well
with love. it is particular . . .
better than exercise
and a big breakfast.
the children go off to school.
the mother goes off to work.
the father and I go out
about our morning
talking
full of painting
          poetry
color
   sun
      words
toward Manhattan.

we have lunch with my father.
my friend likes him.

that makes me feel real good
because
I like him too: he
buys us lunch   tells us
bad jokes / wants us both
to like him. he is afraid
and needs our love. it is
one of those days when
we can all give that
freely.

       after lunch
we go our ways:
I spend the rest of the afternoon
tutoring a student in
the simplest skills of writing.
I do it well today.
he learns from me. when we're finished
he buys me a drink and
another. I am riding high
on everything. it is filling me
and when I meet my friend
again
he is waiting for me
with
     a man we both know
in another bar.
I come in
     feeling so strong
I can hear nothing but
myself. the other man
          is not loving. hears
nothing but himself.
       I am talking
and I burst / all
the love in me dries up.
it's a fever. I can't see them.
there is no love for them
no love for me. I will
       admit nothing
          —no one.
the day is sealed. the talk
becomes
empty.
   I am
angry. I am
amazed how fast I've lost
the day and sit here in
myself.

Situations / 10

for Basil King

our places become our faces.
tonight I was riding the subway
facing ordinary people.
I could see my own face
in the reflection in the window in front of me.
it was a self portrait. suddenly
I saw all my friend's paintings
as a series of self portraits
that he was catching as we
reflected
ourselves
through him (amazing):

the man in
        the big blue hat
                        his lip
        hangs
into his chin
        the big mole on his chin
        is part of his lip
        all part of his blue denim
hat
reflected in his eyes
moves in his body which is
covered
in blue of different shades
—textures. the hands
long
    go
       slowly over into the page
he reads his book joins
at his knee points
back into his nose
                his eyes
are blue are
wandering
next to him to

his left
       the flat brown face

of a young woman her nose
across her face into her eyes
brown almost red (read it in that face
and weep)—it's what she's
worn today—put on
     caught
her face made up so perfect
the tension cracks the corners of
her mouth curl
    she snarls
her tongue curls. her hat is
her hair melts
into her ears—sweet
     perfect
quite perfect eyes that are loud.
she has made herself
perfect. perfect nose that
gives her all away breaks open
her face (breaks open
her heart the key to
her eyes). I wonder if she is able
to smile . . . to his left

past the woman
a double portrait
     two blacks
melt
one checkered—black and white
—greatcoat
    sneakers
his eyes closed his face
moving out his mouth into
his body
    under the coat
no expression as
he talks in that sleep
his face doesn't move but
slides
away from him
     melts
against
into his tight friend
who can't stop moving
      bursts
tight black hair
     blue jacket
worn jeans
pressed with exact fade

his hands moving about
to grab something about to
hold
       these friends hold tight.
then

the fourth down to his left is
the woman whose head is
a pin. she is about to spin
as her smile takes her face
her eyes bright
               sharp as
                        needles
              that head
rests
stuck to
a tight jacket
              dark blue
her blueblack eyes nice
                       neat
that smile hangs
and hangs it is
a strap.
       behind them

in the window I see
my face
       the faces
and lower shoulders of
those who sit around me
in that dark reflection
in fragments that mix this space.
we stare back at
ourselves.

A Necessary Love

for Mallory King

you've taken it
into yourself
and
in that
come into
yourself
      come
among us
        nervous
with love
      —common
to us all
      if we should only
tell it; so
      tonight
the family gathers
around
      the table (for
the evening meal
          for
the stories)—and
          tonight
you sit with us
        you and
your young man
        sharing
in our lives
while
    your sister waits
nervous
      with her glimpse
of things to come
        (the intimacy)
her edge
her need
      holds fiercely
to when you
        were babies together

```
her sense of loss
                her desire
to hold back
                but go there
                                too (fiercely)
not easy at the table
                wanting to be held
rocked in the bosom of
our gathering
                —your father
looking
checking
but giving you
                what is yours
his love
to take
        to heart (talking
to this first
            new love)
your father's
            shy
                need to know
                if
this kid
        is tender too (their shyness
touches in the talk)
                    —your mother
watching
        wondering (wandering)
in her life
        as it is blood
                    with yours
and me (almost
                uncle)
friend
    touched by what you've found
by how
    you've passed
                to here
passing (passing
filling
the days of our lives)
and
there
just then
you get silent
then turn to
me
```

                to tell me
your
        first memory
of me
standing
            over you
as
your father
            bent
to button your yellow
                        raincoats (you
and your sister
                —four and five
and me making
acquaintance)
                —the love
that
    in that
            moment
    got moving
—I see you then
bundled
so lovingly
against
the storm
            —so now
you do it
for yourself
bundled with
our love.

The Wellsprings:
A Suite for Thelonious Monk and Wilhelm Reich

The Wellsprings: A Suite for Thelonious Monk and Wilhelm Reich

Love, work and knowledge are the wellsprings of our life.
They should also govern it.
—Wilhelm Reich

if creation comes through you
it might be years before
you know
        just what
                it is.
—Thelonious Monk
  via Steve McCall (in conversation)

1. the long day

mostly gone now
now sitting
        stark
holding naked
the sun to
      my body
      my body become
a piano
    sun tinkling
            oh . . .
                  like
a ruby
    my dear
a stream:
      the keys strike
clear rays play musics
              gently—the labor held
already
the melody contained
           rolling out—each node
a note of light
each bud

    answers to:
        The Jewel Of Musics

        or

        A Ruby, My Dear

        or

        The Sun Of It All

        or

        A Port In Any Call

2. *on the creative*

        on the train
into a blues . . .
      who's mood's this one?
this one's on me:
      as in an old man's heart
the world seems forever full (but fragile)
the confusion is—who is
      the doctor who
    the father
        's loving care
who knows what a mother knows:

the heart in need
      goes nutty (it is
the little rootie tootie of
      the heart
        you hear
—it's there
  and there
two takes
    off minor):

      they took him to a room
left him (Reich)—
    with his heart broken
to sing life against a prison (well
you
   needn't ask
      what music's)

like
     the piano-player (Monk—alone)
sitting hours
          on end
              under his hat
                    naked in
             his overcoat
making so much song
                  it is not possible
to know for sure (Monk's mood
                    Reich's mood)
is
there now
to make that music
          there and
          there—no
          there is
no obligation (the riddle of
              my solo
                    grows
the answer is:
          Let Me See You

     or

          Say What You Are

     or

          What's Your Name?

     or

          You're Darn Tootin'

     or . . .

3. *the line:*

              the least resistance
no simple song
no melody lingering. most of our lives
the song dies: we are
              compelled:
easier
to demand discipline

```
                        forced march
authority—easier than
                        the musics tingling
in children
        taking their lives as
                        their own
—the pleasure . . .
                let's say it
simply
the best music is
        SEX—*always something for*
        *the lovers* . . . oh
        much easier to crown
                        some Führer
        given by
                some God
                        to tell us
        what we are
                what we think
                        what we do—easier to
        make love
                a legal bind
                        fixed
        easier than
                friendship—the musics of
                                ourselves
                                        easier
        to sell
                one's birth for
        the security of
                        a trap—who wants
        to sing
                a song—mysterious in
        the chords it strikes?—mysterioso:
                                train whistle
        long into
                the heart of
                        the heart of
                train whistle
the matter:
easier to
sing commonplace songs—easier to
stand for
        the commonplace:
it's easier than
creation—it might be years
before
        you know
```

                    just what
                              that is.

4. *conscious action is*
                                        a drop
in the bucket of
the unconscious: and we are
                              afraid to know:
proud of
our fine personalities . . .
                    "such fine
                              individuality"
                    "such
broadness of mind"
                    ain't we fine
                              ain't we
tossed:
weren't we angry
              when we found out
we came down from apes?
                    heartbroken
to learn
        we are not
              the center of the universe . . .
        even
strangers to ourselves? but

look out the window
              —look at
the night
        its musics
              delight
so full of all
        the stars
              we are:

        wink

smile

hum

and let's

cool

one.

5. *the function of the blues*

just a closer walk
                (documented in dreams)
—I mean
the last week
        or two
documentary dreams
—each called
the blues come down
                going
                      going
gone—up there
            I could hear nobody
gone down home
            into sleep where
the musics find their way into
waking
      —rolling
            trembling
    to hold on to
what?
      up here
            —down there
where?
     where?
where?
     —and only in the musics
the blues as such
            are put away
stomped—in the dreams
              whispering
                      a melody:
if you could see me now—where?
only in the musics has
            the animal been touched
in the blues in
        energy
blue energy
        the animal of it
               moaning
long whistle—a closer walk
               moaning
how long that train that dream of love?
—each of us
with hearts like rocks thrown in
the black sea—down there:
where

                where?
where?

where we stomp (first in dreams)
where we hear the musics
                        that make us
dancers—shaking
            (our asses)
stomping
        blue devils:
BLUE DANCING
            blue Monk dancing
blue Reich dancing
            blue Harry
blue dancing in your head—how long
—oh
the train is long
all night in the whistle in
the dark the blues rattle
roll
    little lights
            for us
and in the morning
            the blues still
call for
    the light
call for
    the dance of
            the musics
the animal
        wanting so much
to be touched.

6. *the archaeology of us*

                        rock hard
rigid
    history. every layer
a piece of life
            —strata
when we go into it
            we go down
at each level
            we might find riches
                    and
some curse—so painful

                              we decide
even the sun
                  glow
of life
            a present
                        a day alive
            full of
the world
                  is ugly: strata: when we
go into it
            it can shatter
                              into the
sad face:
            interface
                        covered by a curse
of gray days or
                  by questions: *How Can I Know About
Love
      I Didn't Know About Me?*
                                    or
                              Do You Know What It Means?
                        and if so
      What Can I Do About It?

why not
            touch the animal? take the prehistoric beast of
yourself out into the light layer
                              by layer—sit down
at a table
            in some cafe
consider the point of
                        the light
what it falls on
each layer
            of resistance
a layer of pain—screaming as
it's pulled back
                  careful
                              archaeological
and in that light to live
                              with
your own (each of us
                  our own)
PREHISTORY (again
                  —again):

when the darkhaired pretty young woman
told me she didn't like Reich's idea that we were

all suffering from a disease it was *she insisted* (like
she was challenging me to argue or defend some piece of
music) it was *she insisted* the craziness made people
interesting and fun. the idea of illness was a downer . . .
sad
     but then think *I said* what a healthy person would be
like *I said* the musics are unlimited / no reason
to be afraid to
name the illnesses—so it came back
                                 that way
to Monk—or back to Ellington or
                                 back to Armstrong
(all the years
          the lives
naming the illness)
                 blowing those devils away
funny that way—how easy we can take it when we
can dance to it—or back history (dance with it)
pre-
    and present
to us
       dancing
stomping
           on the layers
of all that pain.—yes: *crazy*
                        they call me
sure I'm crazy
crazy in love
             on
or about—oh
well
     let's call this:

                Sticks And Stones Will Break What's Left
                After The Heart Breaks With Longing
                And Considers Itself Well Taught

                or

                It Ain't Never Been Easy Except
                Before It Got Hard

A Portrait of Wilhelm Reich

I went to sleep
feeling rejected
dreamt all night

                of rejection (curled
pulled
        against myself—angry)
I woke when she woke
feeling rejected when
                she left
                        the bed.

it was later
        in the shower
that it came
        to me: I didn't even know if
I wanted to make love
but wanted her
            to prove
herself to me:

            such confusion
such sadness:
to lose love:
        to know so little of
ourselves. to stop so fully
dead.

🐂

Wilhelm Reich was born
            March 24th, 1897
grew up in
        the German-Ukrainian part of
Austria
        1000 acres
                —three generations of farmers
trying not to be Jews
            covering his
                    isolation:
the suicide of his mother
            the heartbroken
                        death of
            his father
the war in 1917 breaking
            the land
covering it all.
the discovery of nature
            in childhood (alone)
biology:
the harvest:
        the land

the animals

there is that moment
about the naked woods
that winter's
        left
just
    before spring
               breaks full (this year
in these parts
        it's already
               middle May)
when
    it is not covered yet
it is not
    naked still
but still
    so soft
it's sexy
    to take it in.
it is that moment
before
    your lover
pulls
the covers lush
around

1919

perhaps
    it was
        the moralism
    with which
the subject was
        approached . . .
            disturbed him.
from his own experience
        from observations made
on himself
    and others
he reached the conclusion that:

The character structure of modern man, who reproduces
a six-thousand-year-old patriarchal authoritarian culture,
is typified by characterological armoring against his inner

nature and against the social misery which surrounds him. This characterological armoring is the basis of isolation, indigence, craving for authority, fear of responsibility, mystic longing, sexual misery and neurotically impotent rebelliousness, as well as pathological tolerance. Man has alienated himself from, and has grown hostile toward, life. This alienation is not of a biological but of a socio-economic origin. It is not found in the stages of human history prior to the development of patriarchy.

. . . Sexuality is the center around which the life of society as a whole as well as the inner intellectual world of the individual . . . revolves.

after that war
the need for medicine
to heal
        to understand
                      all those wounds:
the University of Vienna
                      1918–1922
did well
       doing the best he could
filling gaps—the rest
                of his life
filling gaps
        starting first with
Freud's sharp knowledge
                      —the opening
into the soul—the link between
life and its illnesses:

Sexual energy operates in the whole body, not just in the tissues of the gonads.

kept on analyzing
                     —but Freud slipped into
the authority of death: giving up
                          giving death
a polite place in
the new age
        —gave up
to fear
       —gave up Reich, and
grew dark
       —like a caged animal
doubting almost everything

it
falls in
on
itself.
collapses
        down
                through
        the psyche
—the soma (body
and soul) into
around
        about
the blood
shrinks into
the nucleus
where the system
caves in
then explodes
                (cell
by cell)
        putting out
the light

Every seemingly arbitrary destructive action is a reaction of the organism to the fustration of a vital need, especially of a sexual need.

                went out to make
a revolution
        of that
                —found Marx:
how much it costs to create
healthy men
                and women—how much
it takes to open us
                —a lifetime
or longer. opened clinics
opened
        discussion—lost
the safety of his profession
                in questions
in examinations
        in speaking to
the lives of
        people lost
his honors
        among his peers
lost his country
        lost his home
escaped the Nazis

>   escaped the Communists
> escaped the psychoanalysts
> found himself first in one place
>   then another
> but found
>   the science
>   the facts
>   that took him
> deeper into
>   the matter.

. . . The longing for love and the fear of genitality are international.

Orgastic potency is the capacity to surrender to the flow of biological energy, free of any inhibitions; the capacity to discharge completely the dammed-up sexual excitation through involuntary pleasurable convulsions of the body. Not a single neurotic is orgastically potent, and the character structures of the overwhelming majority of men and women are neurotic.

Society molds human character. In turn, human character reproduces the social ideology en masse. Thus, in reproducing the negation of life inherent in social ideology, people produce their own suppression.

. . . Cultural happiness in general and sexual happiness in particular are the real content of life, and should be the goal of a practical politics of the people.

The entire politics of culture (film, novels, poetry, etc.) revolve around the sexual element, thrive on its renunciation in reality and its affirmation in the ideal.

. . . The molding of a negative sexual character structure is the real, unconscious goal of education.

Sexual suppression becomes an essential tool of economic enslavement.
Sexual repression is of a socio-economic and not of a biological origin.

The natural instincts are biological facts. They cannot be done away with and they cannot be fundamentally changed.

Freud psychologized biology.

. . . First, . . . there is no biological masochism; second, . . . conformity to present-day reality, e.g., irrational upbringing or irrational politics, is itself neurotic.

The living merely functions. It does not have any "meaning."

tension ⟶ charge ⟶ discharge ⟶ relaxation

The orgasm formula could also be called the "life formula."

The life process consists of continuous alternation between expansion and contraction.

The orgasm reflex is a unitary response of the total body. In the orgasm, we are nothing but a pulsating mass of plasm.

Bioenergetically, the psyche and the soma function as a mutually conditioning as well as a unitary system.

When a strict, sex-negating partriarchy wants to reproduce itself, it must severely suppress the sexual impulses of children.

It is one of the great secrets of mass psychology that the average adult, the average child, and the average adolescent are far more prone to resign themselves to the absence of happiness than to continue to struggle for the joy of life, when the latter entails too much pain. Thus, until the psychic and the social preconditions necessary for vital life have been understood and established, the ideology of happiness must remain mere verbalization.

---

what comes of sleep
                where lovers come
a maze
      of love
amazed
       with love
may
    love's dreams
all dreams
         of lovers come
to haunt my sleep

---

         what is to be done?
except examine
the nature
         the physics of
our energy
         the discovery of
the pulse of life
          our pulse
in
   and through
         the universe
the breakthrough into
           biology
into our needs.

                    Reich discovered the bion
the simplest unit
                    —discovered the charge
the orgone energy—discovered
the fact of self-regulation:
                              trapped in
                                        his science
the clearer it
              became
facing
a world that felt first
                        uncomfortable
then angry—he had not
                      freed them
he could not cure them
                       he made no promise
he became isolated
                   in the clarity of
                                     his science
became frustrated
                  angry with what he knew
should be done . . .
                     went
                          deeper
into
    the science:
                 built a science
that maintained
                the equation between
the highly complicated
                       and the simple.

every charge brought by
                        the Food and Drug Administration
against Reich was contradicted
                               completely by
Reich's and his co-workers' own work
                                     —fabrications
yet
they sent Reich to jail for criminal
contempt. they declared him
mad. they burnt
                his books
they laughed. they
                   remained unhappy

confused. —even his death
                           in 1957
in federal prison
                gave them
                         no resolution
—gave no relief.

The Rich Soil / *The Question* / *The Point*

50 years
         or so (after
                 the fact)
they'll come to your grave
ask you to
        forgive them.
there'll be nothing to forgive . . .

50 years (more
               or
less).

it still won't
        spring the locks:
                  our desire for
masters
      Great Men
              or Women (50 years
100 years)
        after the fact. it's of
little use:
        "Do you know
        what
        Christ
        knew? He knew
        the Life Energy."
               "In a simple way
                he knew about
                the fields and
                the grass and
                babies. That's what
he knew."

when will our children
find their natural lives?
in 50?
in 100? years?

why do we need
scientists
to tell us?
when will poets
sing
      wild
lovely
      plain
            simple
      song
for us?
        in 50?
        in 100?
years?

this is not
epilogue. it is
the world
breathing in
the work
in
these musics.

A Portrait of Thelonius Sphere Monk

first solo:

the musics
          take me
in their weather
cover me
        a river to
the melody
while under the melody
under the keys
under the rhythm
you will see
my heart in
my feet

      DANCING

'Round Midnight
                Who Knows Thelonious?
who knows

Monk's Mood?

musicians play his tunes
but
    can't play
            his style.
his things
       are hard
in all kinds of ways
                Off Minor
                          my dear
               Ruby,
My Dear
Nice Work If You Can Get It
                      my dear
I Mean You
         I mean
Evidence. I mean
Introspection
              Well,
                   You Needn't
All The Things You Are
                are Mysterioso:
took the piano: took jazz
every aspect of it. you can try
                      so many things:
(Lenore
       backwards—Eronel)
Criss Cross
Straight
      No Chaser. Ask Me Now:

he hits the piano with his elbow
because of
          a certain sound he wants
                             to hear
certain chords. you
can't hit that many notes with
                     your hands.

people laugh . . .

second solo:

the melody plays
its way
about love

                love
how could I know about love
I didn't know about
you? I didn't know about me.
the key is
the solo.

Monk's Dream—Sweet
                And Lovely
                            Reflections

Let's Call This
                Blue Monk
never Played Twice
Think Of One and
                We See:

born Rocky Mount
                North Carolina
October 20
            1920
born Theolious
            moved north—Thelonious
his mother figured
            it was right
never figured he'd do
            anything else.
she was with him. he played (music.
always did play) jazz
            —played what his head
                                built
                Rhythm-A-Ning
the tunes came:
            you can't shout out
                                New York
            can't shout out
that sound.
you have to listen for
            yourself. listen:
Ba—lue (ahum)
Balivar Ba-lues-are (Blue
Bolivar Blues)
            Pannonica (who is she?)
some Sophisticated Lady
                and
                    his wife knows
                in that

Crepuscule With Nellie
      Nutty but he
Let A Song Go Out Of My Heart
        A Caravan
in his Mood Indigo in
      his Solitude
Brilliant Corners
    he figures
if it sounds alright to him
       it sounds
alright

it he gets tired
    sitting at
      the piano
he gets up . . .
     that way
he dances the rhythm better

you can see him alone in his
        old neighborhood
listening
   to San Juan Hill:
solo—Memories
    Of You
Remember
Round Lights 'Round Midnight
Functional Reflections
     You Took The Words
Right Out Of My Heart
    I
Surrender, Dear

—*solo:*
Worry Later
Blues For
   Tomorrow
Abide With Me . . .
      maybe you can tell from
a chance remark
     maybe
      a glance away:

it's o.k.
  it's
sweet and lovely
     Body and
Soul

      bye-ya blues
                      Bright Mississippi
it's Between
The Devil And
                    The Deep Blue Sea
Coming
          On The Hudson
                          we see in
Consecutive Seconds
                          everything's alright:

                    Just You
                            Just Me
                  Just
A Glance At Love

                  Monk's Point:

Monk's time
an architect of music
                          building so carefully
strides—cities in each hand
skyscrapers
            buses
                    garbage trucks
                                with rumbles
and flies.

I'm Confessin'
Everything Happens To Me North Of
                              The Sunset.
Ask Me Now:

            if his playing seems
more simple now, maybe
                        that's because
you can listen better . . .

                  but he
just plays

        his own alone
                    always in some
wee small hour making
                a march
like
    an engine's wailing
                his own

       he makes
                a second-line in
                        the City he's built
and sets it all dancing
                  —hup-two-four-four
giggle ease hum
            slow melody line snake side
                            winder
up into
      undulated
              sweet sweet
                    four four
trading fours or
            whatever comes
                    to hand
          the instrument
become him hum
            two four four
become the whole orchestra in that humming on to
and through his own
                and that's his time: see him
dancing in the piano
            hear him
there.

third solo:

the last time I saw him
he looked older. the group
was just
      o.k.
he sat in the center of his piano
moving deeper
            into
the interior of
            the music
but at the end
            when
he came out to play
alone—the audience screamed
their favorites—all
the obvious stuff
              —but then
in the balcony
            the clear voice
of a woman
           settled it

"You play
        whatever you want . . .

maestro"

who knows
what music
          lurks?

the Monk
      knows . . .

trinkle
     tingle.

7. Final

a valentine
       for
          the beat of it.
there's nothing more regular. we are
the drum. we are
         after all
the heart of it all:
         if love comes
               through you
       it might be
a lifetime
      before you know
           just what
              it is
(if ever)—that was work / that was
knowledge / that was creation (who was
                that masked stranger?):

CODA

that is Reich
held until
his heart
broke. the beat
stopped
his books burning
across
the prison floor.

that is Monk
still dancing in
his head—playing
in rumors
in fantastic spells
naked—a smile (caught in
a wink)

        it is
the drum of ourselves
the struggle
out of our heroes
for they are only
alive as
we go from them
the recipe
for the stew:

          something's
cooking in that
stew of energy
in the melody—oh
I love
the taste
the mix—the labor

the picture of me
one year old
pushing up at
the world smiling
—it is not
a mask but
a smile
and down through
that smile
I see
a heart beating:

it is how
one night
I discover
a spider
as it hangs
gliding
weaving
the drum of its life
driven through

the air in
the beat of
its pulse . . .
weaving to make
a net for its
meal
    its
particular stew.

it finishes
and holds
center
    reading
each touch
each piece of food
cooking in
its web

    —beating . . .
its heart
stretched
out on
    each strand
—a full night's work
building re-
    building
the kitchen of
its perfect instinct
food beats
in us.
we are
center in
the stew's web, we
are (each man
woman
    of us)
hatched
and fed
on what
our mothers
could give:

    how
one night
I learned that

there is one spider
who hatches her young
and ends her life
hanging dead center
in her web
becoming
her children's food.
they eat her
up. her heart
beating
until
the end.